ANCIENT *for* PATHS

MODERN WOMEN

Walking with the Lord

JUDY GERRY

LIFESONG
PUBLISHERS

ANCIENT PATHS
MINISTRIES

ISBN   0-9718306-2-2

Published by LifeSong Publishers
P.O. Box 183, Somis, CA 93066-0183
805-655-5644
www.lifesongpublishers.com

Unless otherwise noted, all Bible quotations used in this study are taken from the New American Standard Bible.

Illustrations by Wendy Kappen
Cover design by Jeff Sharpton and Jon Walusiak at Design Point
Printed in the United States of America

First Edition
Library of Congress Control Number: 2003111290
p. 100 cm. 25.4

TABLE OF CONTENTS

Endorsements

"Being born female in today's western world frequently offers a false sense of confidence. Armed with education and unprecedented privilege, women are writing their own scripts about family and personal fulfillment, but later encounter confusion and bleak emptiness. Having been taught to disregard the wisdom of their Creator, they bypass the solutions they seek.

Judy Gerry has dug deeply into the sacred records of the Bible to surface divine guidance for women in every generation. Here is a timely, reassuring and professionally crafted study resource which belongs in every church library and on the study agenda for thinking women."

Howard G. Hendricks
Distinguished Professor and Chairman, Center for Christian Leadership
Dallas Theological Seminary

"Judy Gerry has a long-time track record of walking with the Lord as a woman and as a wife and mother. For many years, she has had an effective ministry of training women in the Word and ways of God. Now her years of study and experience are combined in this practical, interactive course designed to help women understand God's purpose and plan for their lives.

Judy does not claim to offer new or original ideas. Rather, she leads women to discover and apply the tried, true, and enduring way laid out for us in the Scripture– the pathway that leads to blessing and joy.

In a day when so many Christian women are floundering and confused, the wisdom found in this program is timely and desperately needed. I pray this course will be widely received and will be used to bring about a true revolution in the hearts and homes of women who profess to know Christ."

Nancy Leigh DeMoss
Author; Host of Revive Our Hearts Radio

"I love *Ancient Paths for Modern Women* because it takes women to the Bible! His Word changes lives! I have observed tearful testimonies of women coming to Christ, marriages healed, children raised according to God's plan, repentance revived, and church problems solved. Today's women are so thirsty to hear God's Word. After teaching *Ancient Paths* this summer to forty women, I again stand in awe as I have watched God work through this study."

Linda Campbell
Bible Study Leader
Actively Serving in Women's Ministries in Ventura County

Preface

Millennia ago God set out ancient paths for us to walk, which would lead to abundant life, and into perfect fellowship with Himself. The Lord promised us that when we see and walk in that "good way," we will find rest for our souls.

"Thus says the LORD,
'Stand by the ways and see and ask for the ancient paths,
Where the good way is, and walk in it;
And you will find rest for your souls.'"
Jeremiah 6:16

Contemporary women have veered sharply from the "good way" that God has intended for us to live. While longing for elusive rest for their souls, women have rejected God's pathways as being too simplistic and archaic. Sensing that something is wrong, we are unable to grasp how grossly off track we are.

Many Christian women have "stumbled from the ancient paths," by believing various ideas and secular concepts which are not biblical (Jeremiah 18:15). Lives are being diminished by disobedience, and it truly breaks our Father's heart.

Many women are walking in darkness. In order to dispel the darkness, we need to turn on the light. God has told us that His Word will light our path (Psalm 119:105). The goal of this study is to discern God's will for women as we learn what Scripture reveals about women of the Word.

As a young mother in the 1970's, I encountered scores of good Bible studies dealing with being a woman of God. Today there are only a few to be found, yet there is an increasingly dire need for teaching biblical mandates for women.

Through the strong and helpful encouragement of my husband, Dave, and the enthusiastic support of our five children, the Lord led me in preparing this material. Special thanks to the many women who have continually encouraged me, and to Dave who has spent countless hours formatting these materials.

While preparing this study I learned much, and the Lord has used His Word to exhort and challenge me to personal spiritual growth. My prayer is that as you dig into the Word, you will become conformed to the image of Christ.

"For I am confident of this very thing, that He who began a good work in you
will perfect it until the day of Christ Jesus. For it is only right for me to feel this
way about you all, because I have you in my heart..."
Philippians 1:6,7a

Judy

How to Use this Study

During this study we will focus on God's specific directives for women. Taking biblical commands and precepts one by one, our goal will be to determine what God is telling us to do, and to explore how they are practical for the "nitty-gritty" of daily living.

How do women of the Word go about living in this world today? *Ancient Paths for Modern Women* is a four-part discipleship program designed to be most effective when studied in sequence.

- **Ancient Paths I- Walking With the Lord** (seven weeks), addresses how to develop an intimate, personal walk with the Lord.

- **Ancient Paths II- Walking as Wives** (seven weeks), leads us to learn and apply what God says about women walking as wives in the marriage relationship.

- **Ancient Paths III- Walking as Mothers and Homemakers** (seven weeks), examines the Lord's desire for women as they disciple their children and build God-honoring homes

- **Ancient Paths IV- Walking in the Church and in the World** (eight weeks), grapples with issues related to God's will for women in the church, a woman's walk in the secular world, and how to keep walking faithfully.

It is preferable to have each chapter's work completed prior to the Bible study time. Many chapters have questions marked "***Optional***". If you choose to answer those questions you will need additional Bible study resource books. A description of these is located at the back of this study.

You will notice that each page has a "Prayer Points" area provided in the margin. This is designed for use in jotting down ideas, items for discussion, questions, group prayer requests, or personal prayer needs that the Holy Spirit may bring to mind during the study.

The last page of each chapter is best handled in a small group format. It is recommended that you complete and record your "Summary," "Discussion" and "Application" responses prior to the lesson so that you can share your answers and ideas.

It is suggested that you use the chapter heading as a type of filing system. It may be a notebook with pockets or a portable file. As time goes by, insert current events, magazine articles, and even cartoons, into the appropriate chapter topic. Be alert for other applicable Scripture to insert in various chapters. The long-term goal is that you will be able to teach and encourage other women as you mature in the Lord using the enclosed materials.

⌘   ⌘   ⌘

Ancient Paths Bible Study Series is especially effective when used by "older women" as they mentor "younger women." The long-term goal of this study is that you will be able to teach and encourage other women as you both mature in the Lord.

"Come, Walk the Ancient Paths"

Come and walk the ancient paths	(Jeremiah 6:16)
That lead into the Savior's heart.	(Revelation 19:7)
His Word reveals the wisdom past	(Proverbs 4:11)
Of just one Way to life and rest,	(John 14:6)
So choose this route and start.	(Deuteronomy 30:19)
Come, walk the road that leads to joy,	(Psalm 16:11)
And though the trail may steepen,	(James 1:2)
The obstacles of Satan's ploys	(Ephesians 6:10-13)
Thrust us on Jesus to employ	(II Corinthians 12:9, 10)
His grace, which daily deepens.	(Hebrews 4:16)
Come, run by grace, the ancient race,	(Hebrews 12:1)
Intent to win the prize.	(I Corinthians 9:24)
The goal in view is Jesus' face;	(Hebrews 12:1)
Press on, reach out, pick up the pace	(Philippians 3:13, 14)
Toward heaven set your eyes.	(Hebrews 12:2)
Then stand before the Bema Seat	(II Corinthians 5:10)
Rewarded by the Son.	(II Timothy 4:8)
To place our crowns back at His feet	(Revelation 4:10)
Will be our joy. Our prize most sweet	(Philippians 4:1)
To hear Him say, "Well done."	(Matthew 25:21)
Be seated in the heavenly places	(Ephesians 2:6)
With Christ, forever home.	(Revelation 21:3)
Our walk by faith, and zeal of race,	(II Corinthians 5:6, 7)
Will show the riches of His grace	(II Timothy 4:7)
In ages yet to come.	(Ephesians 2:7)
Come, walk the ancient paths.	(Jeremiah 6:16)

Judy Gerry

UNIT ONE

WALK IN THE
RIGHT DIRECTION

**"This is what the Lord says:
'Stand in the crossroads and look for the ancient paths,
ask where the good way is, and walk in it,
and you will find rest for your souls.'"
Jeremiah 6:16**

Unit I Chapters:

Get On The Right Track

Receiving Jesus Christ as my personal Savior and
determining to follow the path that
He has designed for my life.

**"Enter through the narrow gate; for the gate is wide
and the way is broad that leads to destruction, and
there are many who enter through it. For the gate is
small and the way is narrow that leads to life, and
there are few who find it."
Matthew 7:13, 14**

Prayer Points:

"Enter through the narrow gate; for the gate is wide and the way is broad that leads to destruction, and there are many who enter through it. For the gate is small and the way is narrow that leads to life, and there are few who find it."
Matthew 7:13, 14

I. Two Diverging Roads

"The Road Not Taken"

Two roads diverged in a yellow wood,
And sorry I could not travel both
And be one traveler, long I stood
And looked down one as far as I could
To where it bent in the undergrowth.

Then took the other, as just as fair,
And having perhaps the better claim,
Because it was grassy and wanted wear;
Though as for that the passing there
Had worn them really about the same,

And both that morning equally lay
In leaves no step had trodden black
Oh, I kept the first for another day!
Yet knowing how way leads on to way,
I doubted if I should ever come back.

I shall be telling this with a sigh
Somewhere ages and ages hence:
Two roads diverged in a wood, and I -
I took the one less traveled by,
And that has made all the difference.

(Robert Frost)

Poets have written about it, songs have been sung about it, books have been written about it, and mothers have lectured their children about it since time began. Men innately sense in their spirit that the path which they choose in life bears great eternal significance.

Every person makes a choice. Today, whether you are conscious of it or not, you are on a road which you have selected. Unlike the view of the above poet, who felt that both paths had merit, God's Word states that all paths are not created equal. As the above poet could not see where the two paths led, our Creator describes two paths and the destination of those roads. Jesus speaks of the two path choices in life that are vastly different.

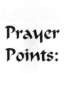

1. Look up the following verses and complete the chart to see how Scripture contrasts these two paths.

Scripture	Path #1 - Good	Path #2 - Evil
Matthew 7:13,14	Narrow gate Narrow way Few find it	Wide gate Broad way leads to destruction Many enter by it
Psalm 1:1-6		
Proverbs 2:11-15		
Jeremiah 6:16		
Psalm 84:5		
Isaiah 59:7,8		
Psalm 77:13		
Proverbs 16:17		
Proverbs 4:18		Proverbs 4:19
Proverbs 14:12, 16:25		
Proverbs 12:28		

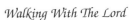

Prayer Points:

2.   Based upon your answers and insights from studying the previous verses, draw a picture of your interpretation of the "two roads" described in the Bible. (OK, this won't be graded! Stick figures are fine!) Be creative!

(If possible, draw yourself into this picture indicating where you are located on these two roads. If you are unsure which road you are currently traveling, feel free to leave it blank, or perhaps draw yourself at the crossroads of these paths.)

II. Determine Your Destination

Millennia ago God set out ancient paths for us to walk which would lead us into perfect fellowship with Himself, and perfect fulfillment in our lives. It was "the good way" (Jeremiah 6:16a).

Thus says the LORD,
"Stand by the ways and see and ask for the ancient paths,
Where the good way is, and walk in it;
And you will find rest for your souls."

Does the path on which you are walking meet God's criterion as the "good one," the one for which you were uniquely created? Are you truly contented and is your soul at rest?

Or do you find yourself, like most women in our culture, frustrated with what you are doing, having no idea of where you are headed? Having rejected God's pathway as being too simplistic and archaic, have you been detoured from pathway to pathway in pursuit of elusive satisfaction from something new and different, only to wind up going around in circles in the rocky cul-de-sac of life?

Perhaps you find yourself in a third group of women, those who are uncertain of what road they are traveling.

Generations of mankind have come and gone, each attempting to design their own pathways to fulfillment. Today we find ourselves, both as a society and as individuals, having veered intensely from those ancient paths. Having stubbornly rebuffed God's good way, we know that something is wrong but seem unable to grasp how grossly off track we are. We are groping in darkness, unaware of what questions to ask which would lead us back on course.

In order to get back on the right track we need to ask, "Where am I going in life? What is my purpose or destination?" When your life comes to an end, what is it that you hope to have seen accomplished?

3.   Take a moment right now and prayerfully note any personal life goal(s) that come to mind.

    a)

Prayer Points:

b)

c)

God has revealed, in His Word, the destination of the ancient path that He has designed for us. Unlike the poet who could not see past where the road bent in the undergrowth, God's Word gives us clear vision of where the "good way" will take us.

4.   Look up the following verses and note the destination and goal of those who follow God's paths.

   a)   John 14:2-4

   b)   Philippians 3:10, 11

   c)   Philippians 3:12-14

   d)   Isaiah 35:8-10 (Jeremiah 50:5; Psalms 84:5)

   e)   Hebrews 11:16

   f)   Hebrews 12:1, 2

   g)   Revelation 21:2, 3

5. Note what the following verses say about what will happen when the "good way" traveler arrives at his destination.

    a)   Matthew 25:21

    b)   II Timothy 2:15

    c)   II Timothy 4:7, 8

    d)   Revelation 3:4

6. God loves us so much that He not only promises eternal reward for us in heaven, He gives us promises for the here-and-now part of that journey on earth. What does He promise for daily living?

    a)   John 10:10

    b)   Jeremiah 1:8

    c)   Jeremiah 6:16

    d)   Matthew 28:20

Prayer Points:

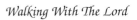

III. Choose Your Route

The Lord makes it clear that we choose which of the two roads we will take. It is not a question of circumstance or good fortune, it is an issue of our spirit and our will; we all make a choice.

7. Read Deuteronomy 30:15, 19, 20. Describe what choice is set before you:

Which road will you follow? What choice do you make?

IV. The Path Is a "Toll Road"

Making an intellectual decision to follow God's paths is the first step toward walking with God. However, simply making a mental decision to walk God's way will lead to failure and frustration since none of us can possibly live up to God's qualifications in our own strength. Perfect holiness, being clean before God, is a prerequisite for walking His ways. The problem is that none of us can qualify because we are all sinners. Sin is failure to meet God's perfect standards of holiness through either being passively indifferent or actively rebellious toward Him. God is holy, and though we were created to have fellowship with God, our independent self-will broke this union.

There is a penalty for sin. A price must be paid before we are allowed passageway on this road which leads into the Lord. Much like a toll way, the cost is predetermined and exact. The cost is the blood and death of a perfect sacrifice.

God loves us so much, and desires intimate friendship with us. Because we are unable to pay this "entry fee" He took the burden upon Himself and sent Jesus, His only Son, to die for us. Jesus Christ is God's only provision for mans' sin.

Intellectually agreeing with all of this is not enough, we must act upon it. Even the demons (intellectually) believe in Jesus (James 2:19). We must receive Jesus Christ as our personal Lord and Savior; turning to God from self (repenting), and asking Him to come into our lives to forgive our sins and to make us the women that He wants us to be. Walking in God's way is a spiritual decision.

8. God's truth is contrary to human reasoning and contemporary thought. Complete the following chart that contrasts Satan's lies with God's truth.

Satan's Lies	God's Truth
There are many paths to God.	John 14:6
Man is basically good.	Romans 3:10 Romans 3:23 Isaiah 53:6
God won't judge sin.	John 3:36 Romans 6:23
My good deeds outweigh my bad ones.	Isaiah 64:6 Ephesians 2:8,9
"Salvation" comes by having faith in ourselves, not by having faith in a supernatural power.	Romans 10:9.10
Our life on earth never ends; we are reincarnated.	Hebrews 9:27
We can't be sure we are going to heaven	Romans 8:16 1 John 5:13

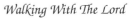

Prayer Points:

9.   Jesus Christ paid the purchase price for us (I Corinthians 6:20). Look up the following verses and find out what He bought, and what was the cost .

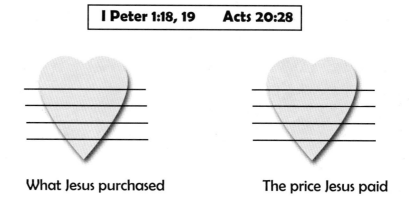

| I Peter 1:18, 19   Acts 20:28 |

What Jesus purchased   The price Jesus paid

Scripture says:

"But as many as received Him, to them He gave the right to become children of God" (John 1:12). And "Whoever believes in Him shall not perish, but have eternal life" (John 3:16).

10.   Have you ever received Christ as your personal Savior? If so, take a moment and briefly record the events surrounding that decision in your life.

If you have never received Christ why not ask Him into your life now? Talk with God, acknowledge that you are a sinner in need of Jesus' salvation, and ask Him into your heart. The moment that you do that, several things happen:

a)   Christ comes into your life (Colossians 1:27)
b)   You are forgiven of all your sins (Colossians 1:14)
c)   You become a new creation (II Corinthians 5:17)
d)   You receive eternal life (John 5:24)
e)   You become a child of God (John 1:12)

11.   If you asked Christ into your life to be your Savior today, record and describe your decision below. It will encourage you in the days ahead.

Prayer Points:

Once we receive the free gift of God, salvation through Christ's blood, we begin the great adventure on that road of life for which we were created. Though we may be tempted to veer off of the pathway on this journey, we can never lose our salvation because Jesus will never leave us or forsake us (Hebrews 13:5).

The early Christians considered being on this pathway so precious that they called themselves followers of "The Way" (Acts 9:2; 22:4; 24:14, 22).

> "I shall be telling this with a sigh
> Somewhere ages and ages hence:
> Two roads diverged in a wood, and I—
> I took the one less traveled by,
> And that has made all the difference."

Prayer Points:

SUMMARY:

Define "receiving Jesus Christ" in your own terms. You could use a synonym, a motto, a poem or prayer, or even make a drawing to show your understanding of this phrase.

DISCUSSION:

Contemporary thought suggests that all religions lead to God. Will a women who is sincere in her faith, though she does not know Christ as her personal Savior, go to heaven? Why, or why not?

APPLICATION:

A friend of yours says that she would like to become a follower of Christ, but that she's not yet good enough. She says that she will become a Christian after she cleans up her life. What counsel would you give to her?

CHAPTER TWO

STAY ON THE RIGHT TRACK

Continually choosing to follow the path that
Jesus Christ has designed for my life.

"'For My people have forgotten Me,
They burn incense to worthless gods
And they have stumbled from their ways,
From the ancient paths,
To walk in bypaths, Not on a highway'"
Jeremiah 18:15

I. We've Strayed From the Path

**Prayer
Points:**

When we receive Jesus Christ as our Lord and Savior, we begin that journey with Him for which we were created. We start walking the ancient paths He designed which lead to holiness and intimacy with Himself.

There are many obstacles along the way which can tempt us, distract us, and even lead us off course as we seek to follow the Lord. Thousands of years ago God was grieved to note this in His people.

> **"'They burn incense to worthless gods
> And they have stumbled from their ways,
> From the ancient paths,
> To walk in bypaths, Not on a highway'"
> Jeremiah 18:15**

We may go along for awhile, dabbling in paths of disobedience or lingering in side paths of sin. We may successfully hide it from other people, and we hope that God doesn't notice. We may even deceive ourselves into believing that the bypaths aren't so bad.

But what does Scripture say?

1.   Psalm 139:1-3

2.   Isaiah 55:6-9

II.   Get the Map

When we discover that we have veered from the path the first thing that we should do is get the map. Not all maps are accurate. Only one map is the true one.

God has lovingly given us a map that shows us the correct pathway to follow. That map is called the Bible. The word "Bible" literally means "the Book," and it is the only true instruction book for life. Similar to an "owner's manual," our Creator tells us "everything we need for life and godliness" in His holy Word (II Peter 1:3).

God even refers to His commandments and ways as a "plumb line" (Amos 7:8). A plumb line is a cord suspending a weight, which is used to determine vertical direction. Much like a compass works on the horizontal, the plumb line verifies vertical accuracy.

God says that His people are to "ask for the way to Zion turning their faces in its direction" (Jeremiah 50:5). In other words, we're to get out our maps in order to find our way back home.

In this study we will only use God's Word as our source for direction.

III. Let's Retrace Our Steps to the Point Where We Lost Our Way

Just as one who is lost in a maze must retrace his steps to determine the point where he took a wrong turn, it behooves us to retrace our own steps when we discover that we are veering from the road that the Lord has called us to follow.

3.   Has there been anything in your life that has enticed you to leave the right path? Where did you begin to stray? If you can, identify a point along the way where you made a wrong turn or got off course.

God's Word indicates many factors in our lives which may encourage us to detour from His ways. Read the following Scriptures and determine what some of those factors may be.

4.   Proverbs 4:14; I Corinthians 15:33

5.   I Kings 15:26; 22:52

6.   Isaiah 3:12 (Jeremiah 50:6; Malachi 2:7, 8; Galatians 5:7-10)

Prayer Points:

7.   Proverbs 12:15 (Proverbs 14:12; 21:2)

8.   Isaiah 30:9-11; Amos 8:11

9.   Proverbs 22:28 (Deuteronomy 19:14; 27:17)

How do you think the terms "ancient boundary" or "landmark" might apply to contemporary life?

10.   Have you ever stumbled from the right path because of any of the above factors?   If so, which ones do you sense are the greatest threat to your ability to stay on the right track?

11.   What changes can you make in your life to avoid these pitfalls in the future?

IV.   Get Back on the Path

The Lord helps us to realize that we have strayed from the right way, not to torture us, but because He loves us. He wants to enjoy fellowship with us. He greatly desires that we return to the right path and He tells us how to return to Him.

Look up the following verses and record any insights.

12.   Acknowledge that we have stumbled (confess) and repent:

    a)   Isaiah 30:15, 21

    b)   Psalm 119:37

13.   Commit self to Lord and obey His direction:

    a)   Proverbs 3:5, 6

    b)   Psalm 37:5

    c)   Psalm 119:33 (Proverbs 23:19; Psalm 86:11)

14.   Ask Lord for personal guidance:

    a)   Isaiah 48:17

    b)   Psalm 16:11 (Psalm 23:1-3; 5:8; 25:4-8; 27:11; 32:8)

15.   Study the Word (our map)   Psalm 119:35, 105

Prayer Points:

Prayer Points:

V.   Stay on the Path

Our goal in the Christian life is to get on the right pathway and to stay on it. That is where we find true fullness of joy and abundant living.

Once we are on the right road, how do we stay on it? How do we keep from straying and falling off continually? God has given us some insights through His Word on these questions:

16.   Rebuild the pathway. More often than not we find that the road is not an easy one to follow. Often, the path seems to be obscured. What instruction does the Lord give?

   a)   Isaiah 58:12

   b)   Isaiah 62:10

   c)   Jeremiah 31:21

   Are there any specific ways in which you can apply the above verses to your life?

17.   Watch our step. Proverbs 4:26, 27.

18.   Realize that we're pleasing God.

   a)   Colossians 1:10

   b)   Psalm 37:23

19.   Expect opposition from others.

   a)   Proverbs 29:27

   b)   Isaiah 59:15

   c)   Amos 5:10

   d)   Isaiah 51:7 (I Peter 4:3-5)

   Tell about a time when you experienced opposition as
   you determined to be obedient to God.

   How did you respond?

   Which verse(s) above tells us how to respond to
   opposition?

20.   Remember what is at stake.   Deuteronomy 11:26-28.

Prayer Points:

Prayer Points:

21. If you desire to get on the right road and to stay on the path that the Lord has planned for you, take a moment and write out a prayer of thanksgiving and commitment to Him.

In the coming weeks, we will be going step by step along this pathway together as we learn how to walk with the Lord in every aspect of our lives. As we are committed to obedience to Him and His Word, He will faithfully lead us. Let's get started!

Prayer Points:

SUMMARY:

Define "staying on the right path" in your own terms. You could use a synonym, a motto, a poem or prayer, or even make a drawing to show your understanding of this phrase.

DISCUSSION:

Do you think that it is more difficult to live a righteous Christian life today than it was in previous generations? Why or why not?

APPLICATION:

A friend of yours confides that she is unhappy and frustrated in her Christian life. While she says that she wants to live in a way that pleases the Lord, you have observed that she continually makes poor choices that lead her in the opposite direction. She asks you why it is that she is not experiencing "the abundant life" that Christ promised. What do you say to her?

UNIT TWO

WALK WITH THE LORD

**"Therefore as you have received
Christ Jesus the Lord, so walk in Him,"
Colossians 2:6**

Unit II Chapters:

3. Fear the Lord - Proverbs 31:30

4. Cultivate a Gentle Spirit - I Peter 3:4

5. Nurture a Quiet Spirit - I Peter 3:4

6. Be Dignified - Proverbs 31:25

7. Be Reverent in Behavior - Titus 2:3

CHAPTER THREE

FEAR THE LORD

A continual awareness that God is watching and weighing every one of my thoughts, words, actions and attitudes.

**"Charm is deceitful and beauty is vain,
But a woman who fears the LORD,
she shall be praised."
Proverbs 31:30**

**"Charm is deceitful and beauty is vain,
But a woman who fears the LORD, she shall be praised."
Proverbs 31:30**

Prayer Points:

Once we are sure that we are on the correct pathway, we can begin the journey for which God created us. We can begin walking with Him.

What does it mean to "walk with God?" We find the first mention of people walking with God in the first book of the Bible. Look up the following verses.

1.   Genesis 5:22-24

2.   Hebrews 11:5

Based upon these two references, what insights can you draw regarding what it means to walk with God?

Optional: Look up "walked" as used in the above verses, in a concordance and in an expository dictionary. How is the word defined?

What implications might the word "walking" have other than moving upright on one's feet?

Walking with God speaks of cultivating a relationship with God. The result of having a close relationship with the Lord is behavior which pleases Him. Today we will be delving into the first aspect of walking with the Lord- cultivating a relationship with Him.

The first step toward knowing our Lord intimately is to begin to fear Him. Proverbs 9:10 states that "the fear of the Lord is the beginning of wisdom, and knowledge of the Holy One is understanding." The book of Proverbs tells us that "a woman who fears the Lord shall be praised." There was a time not long ago when it was a compliment to refer to someone as being "God-fearing." This is a counter-culture view today.

Many in the churches today relegate the "fear of the Lord" to Old Testament teaching, claiming that it does not apply to the church today since "perfect love casts out fear" (I John 4:18). They maintain that after Jesus came there was no need to fear God. But is this an accurate view of Scripture?

What do you learn about how the early Christians feared the Lord in the following verses?

3.   Acts 9:31

4.   I Peter 1:17

5.   I Peter 2:17

6.   Philippians 2:12

Though some Bible translations substitute the term "reverence" in place of "fear" in the above passages, the same Greek word is used in all of them.

Prayer Points:

Prayer Points:

Optional: Using your concordance or expository dictionary, look up the word "fear" as used in the above passages. How is this Greek word defined?

7.   Let's look at an example from the Old Testament. Read Isaiah 11:3. Someone is described in this passage as "delight(ing) in the fear of the LORD." Of Whom is the writer speaking?

If Jesus Himself, as a Man on earth, delighted in fearing the Lord, is there any reason that we should not have the same attitude?

8.   Read Romans 3:18. Why are all men condemned?

Scripture uses the term "fear of God" in two very different ways: one is of terror and dread, and the other is of reverence and awe. There is a delicate interplay between both of these definitions as applied to the lives of believers. Though as children of God we are delivered from fear of God's wrath I John 4:18), we continue to be faced with the reality of His loving discipline when we sin (Hebrews 12:9-11).

Paul speaks of our relationship to God as being one where we can approach Him crying "Abba, Father" (Romans 8:15) and he also tells us that God "dwells in unapproachable light" (I Timothy 6:16).

9.   Do you have trouble reconciling these two seemingly opposing concepts of God?

One of the reasons that we have lost our healthy fear of God is that we have lost sight of Who God actually is. Our culture has adopted a casual attitude toward the Creator that is in no way biblical. As we travel down the ancient paths with the Lord, we need to know Him in order to know how to relate to Him.

We usually get to know a person by:

     a)   Spending time observing that person,
     b)   Listening to what he says,
     c)   Sharing our heart and thoughts with him.

In a similar way, we get to know the Lord by:

     a)   Spending time observing His works and creation,
     b)   Hearing what He says through His Word,
     c)   Sharing our heart and thoughts with Him through prayer.

Let's listen to what He says. What do the following verses reveal about Who God is?

10.   Isaiah 40:12-26

11.   Isaiah 6:1-8

12.   Hebrews 12:28, 29

13.   Revelation 1:17, 18

**Prayer
Points:**

14.   Revelation 5:12-14

Do you sense a fear indicating terror, a fear indicating love, or a combination of the two in the above verses?

A holy fear of the living God is a prerequisite to true worship. In Exodus 15 the Israelites came before God singing a beautiful song of deliverance extolling the greatness and majesty of God.

15.   Read Exodus 14:31. What specific experiences did the Israelites have that directly preceded and motivated their jubilant song of praise found in Exodus 15?

Christians who have an accurate perception and fear of God are the only people who can truly appreciate God's love. When we see the infinite gulf between a holy God and sinful man, we are overwhelmed by the love God demonstrated for us when He sent His only Son to bridge that gap. There are many aspects to God's love, but it was vividly demonstrated in sending Jesus to die for our sins.

Fearing the Lord enables us to appreciate the salvation of God through Christ accurately. Only then can we truly sense the depth of His love, and sacrifice, for us individually.

Not only will a correct concept of the fear of God cause us to worship God properly, it will also regulate our conduct. It has been said that what or whom we worship determines our behavior.

How does fearing God influence our behavior? Look up the following reference verses and note your answers.

16.   Deuteronomy 6:1, 2

17.   Exodus 20:20

18.   Psalm 111:10

19.   Psalm 130:3, 4

20.   Ecclesiastes 12:13, 14

21.   II Corinthians 7:1

22.   Ephesians 5:21

Our degree of worship and obedience to His Word is a barometer of the level of healthy fear that we have for the Lord. In light of the above passages, would you say that your life exhibits a healthy fear of God?

What areas may need some improvement?

Prayer Points:

23. Check any steps below that you intend to take in order to get to know your Lord more intimately.

☐ I purpose to listen to Him more intently (study Bible).

☐ I purpose to speak with Him more regularly (pray).

☐ I purpose to acknowledge His power and majesty more in life as I observe His hand in the world around me.

☐

☐

Spend some time in prayer acknowledging to the Lord that He, alone, is worthy to be "feared." Confess to Him any area(s) of your life that you recognize where you have not been "fearing" Him appropriately. Ask the Lord to develop the quality of godly fear in your life. Thank God for His great love for you, for the privilege of being His child, and for the joy of walking with Him. Then, commit to the Lord that through His strength you will begin to take obedient action in pursuing true intimacy with Him.

SUMMARY:

Define "fearing the Lord" in your own terms. You could use a synonym, a motto, a poem or prayer, or even make a drawing to show your understanding of this character trait.

Prayer Points:

DISCUSSION:

Ask someone who has walked with the Lord for many years if they notice a change in the way that we "fear the Lord" today as compared with the past. Note any insights.

APPLICATION:

If a woman came to you questioning the value of "fearing God," what would you say to her?

CHAPTER FOUR

CULTIVATE
A GENTLE SPIRIT

A kindness arising from within
that is patiently considerate of others.

"Your adornment must not be merely external—braiding the hair,
and wearing gold jewelry, or putting on dresses; but let it be the
hidden person of the heart, with the imperishable quality of a
gentle and quiet spirit, which is precious in the sight of God."
I Peter 3:3, 4

Prayer Points:

"Your adornment must not be merely external—braiding the hair, and wearing gold jewelry, or putting on dresses; but let it be the hidden person of the heart, with the imperishable quality of a gentle and quiet spirit, which is precious in the sight of God."
I Peter 3:3,4

After we commit ourselves to following Christ's ways in our lives, and sense a healthy "fear of God" as we recognize His great love for us, a natural result is that we desire to please Him.

As we study God's will for women, we discover that the qualities of a gentle and quiet spirit are attributes which God finds precious in women. These qualities are often discussed as one single characteristic. However, though there is strong interplay between these two qualities, they are two very distinct attributes.

Rarely does one hear another praying for God to develop the quality of gentleness in her own life. Yet, the Lord tells us that the trait of being gentle is of great value. He tells us that the trait of gentleness is one of the qualities evidenced by heavenly wisdom [James 3:17], and that when we are maturely walking in a right relationship with Him, gentleness will be manifested in our lives as a fruit of the Spirit [Galatians 5:22, 23].

He especially treasures this gentleness in women.

What does God's Word tell us about how much He values gentleness? Look up the following reference verses and note your observations.

1.   Matthew 5:5: What is the reward for a gentle, or "meek" person?

2.   Matthew 11:29

3.   Matthew 21:5 Of Whom were the prophets Isaiah and Zechariah speaking?

4.   II Corinthians 10:1

5.   I Peter 3:1-5: Who is being exhorted to gentleness?

What adornment is visible?

What adornment is not visible?

How is this attribute visible to God?

How long will this quality last?

When God tells us that a woman's gentle spirit is precious to Him, He is literally saying that He views gentleness as being of the highest possible value or worth.

Knowing that gentleness is desirable; resulting in blessing, and that Christ Himself exemplified this, the question arises; what does it mean to be gentle? When you think of the term "gentle," describe the specific picture that comes to your mind:

According to **Webster's New World College Dictionary**, "gentle" means the following:

a)   *belonging to the upper classes, or polite society*
b)   *like or suitable to polite society; refined, courteous, etc.*
c)   *noble; chivalrous (a 'gentle knight')*
d)   *generous; kind ('gentle reader')*
e)   *easily handled; tame (a 'gentle dog')*
f)   *kindly; serene; patient (a 'gentle disposition')*
g)   *not violent, harsh, or rough (a 'gentle tap,' a 'gentle rebuke')*
h)   *gradual (a 'gentle slope')*

Prayer Points:

In order to understand the meaning of a term, it can be helpful to consider the antonyms, or opposites, of that word. Using the above dictionary definitions as a guideline, write out the "opposite definitions" of "gentle"; what "gentle" is NOT.

a.

b.

c.

d.

e.

f.

g.

h.

Optional: Look up the word "gentle" in your concordance or expository dictionary. (Hint: the word for gentle is sometimes translated "meek" in certain versions of the Bible.) How is the word "gentle" defined?

A gentle person is one who possesses an inward grace of the soul. Demonstrating moderation and patience, a gentle person is always cooperative and considerate of others.

Our culture tends to erroneously associate gentleness with an inert wimpiness that bears no resemblance to the biblical picture of being gentle. Gentleness is not weakness; it is strength under control.

In addition to being manifested in the life of Jesus Christ, what are other pictures of gentleness portrayed in Scripture?

6.   Isaiah 40:10, 11

7.   I Thessalonians 2:5-9

Gentleness differs from a closely related quality of meekness. While gentleness emphasizes the active way which we should treat others, meekness is more a passive trait, describing the correct response of a Christian when mistreated by others. Neither word implies weak inaction.

Some mistakenly interpret gentleness as being born of weakness and a sign of timidity.

8.   Read Psalm 18:30-35. List all of the strong adjectives and descriptions of God the Father:

        a.

        b.

        c.

        d.

        e.

        f.

        In verse 35 what word is used to describe God's strength?

Another mistake that we often make is in assuming that gentleness is an inherited personality trait. We erroneously assume that some Christians are simply "born" gentle, while others are not.

9.   In Galatians 5:22,23, Who is the Source of gentleness?

Prayer Points:

We know that every believer is indwelt by God's Holy Spirit (I Corinthians 6:19; Romans 8:9). The Spirit works in the life of every child of God. We make a mistake if we assume that Christians have the option of selecting their favorite fruit of the Spirit as they ignore others. The fruit of the Spirit is a single cohesive unit. None of the attributes can be ignored.

Some may argue that we don't have the "personality type" conducive to certain behaviors which God desires to manifest in every believer. All of us have strengths and weaknesses, but all of God's Word applies to all of us. The Lord will display His power, and change us, in the areas of our greatest weakness (II Corinthians 12:9, 10).

With whom is gentleness associated?

10.　　I Timothy 3:2, 3

11.　　I Peter 2:18

12.　　II Timothy 2:24, 25

13.　　Titus 3:1, 2

Are YOU to be gentle?

Would those closest to you say that you are a woman with a gentle spirit?

What if you are not a gentle woman? What if you are one of those people who tend by nature to be aggressive toward others, abrupt, inconsiderate, or an insensitive, "tell-it-like-it-is" kind of woman? What if you tends to dominate others with your forceful personality, bluntness, and perhaps intimidation? What should you do if you are leaving a trail of broken bodies in your wake as you travel through life?

We need to begin by recognizing any lack of gentleness in our lives as being disobedience to the Lord. Disobedience is sin.

A lack of gentleness is usually an indication of selfish pride. Gentleness goes out the door when we demand, and fight for, our perceived "rights." In order to be gentle we must humble ourselves and yield our expectations to the Lord. We must be willing to accept His will for us, moment by moment, even when things are not going as we might choose.

A lack of gentleness actually indicates a basic lack of faith. We simply don't believe that everything happening in our life is allowed by God for our good. We don't believe that the Lord is able to help us handle all situations. We tend to become "un-gentle" when we inwardly think, "If I don't make it happen for myself, it won't happen."

A lack of gentleness may also be an indication that we are harboring a bitter attitude toward something, or someone, in our life. Bitterness will cause us to expect the worst in others, and develop a critical, defensive mindset. We will become angry people. A gentle spirit requires that we confess our sins of anger and unresolved bitterness.

If we do not have a gentle spirit, the Lord can change us, and it is possible for us to experience that gentle spirit that He desires for our lives.

What do the following Scriptures tell us about attaining this precious quality of being gentle?

14.　　Colossians 3:12

15.　　I Timothy 6:11

Would you say that being gentle is something that "happens to" us, or is it a choice that we make?

Becoming a gentle woman involves more than just wishing it was so. We must admit our own failure in this area, ask for the Holy Spirit's empowering grace to enable us to become gentle (Galatians 5:22), and then we must cooperate with the Lord by working at it!

Prayer Points:

Paul exhorts Timothy to actively, physically pursue gentleness. A few chapters earlier Paul exhorts Timothy to "discipline yourself for the purpose of godliness" (I Timothy 4:7). Becoming what God wants us to be takes desire and personal effort, but even with intense self-discipline it cannot happen apart from the Holy Spirit working in us (Philippians 2:12, 13).

16. Philippians 4:5 reads,

"Let your gentle spirit be known to all men. The Lord is near."

What do you think that Paul means by this verse? Does the promise that we will see Him soon affect your answer?

17. Prayerfully consider the quality of gentleness in your own life. Can you think of any specific area of your life that needs to be yielded to the Lord where gentleness is lacking?

      a)   in your relationships at home?

      b)   in the way that you deal with your family when you're tired?

      c)   in your relationships and attitudes at church?

      d)   when someone is unkind to your child?

      e)   while you're waiting in a long checkout line at the store?

      f)   when you read the newspaper and troublesome current events?

Do you respond gently? Is your gentle, "forbearing spirit" known to all men?

As you consider the quality of gentleness in your life, note one specific area where you purpose to "put on a heart of... gentleness" (Colossians 3:12).

Prayer Points:

Write out a prayer of commitment to God, asking Him to develop in your heart this "imperishable quality of a gentle... spirit, which is precious in the sight of God. (NIV)"

Prayer Points:

SUMMARY:

Define "having a gentle spirit" in your own terms. You could use a synonym, a motto, a poem or prayer, or even make a drawing to show your understanding of this character trait.

DISCUSSION:

Do you think that the feminist movement in America has affected our concept of being gentle as women? Note any insights.

APPLICATION:

For married women:
A young mother refuses to discipline her children. When asked why, she responds that speaking harshly, as well as physically correcting a child, is not an example of being gentle. How would you counsel this woman?

For single women:
A successful single career woman is struggling with the issue of having a gentle spirit. She wants to know how it is possible to mesh gentleness with the imperative of being an aggressive "mover and shaker" in the workplace. How would you respond to this woman?

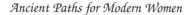

CHAPTER FIVE

NURTURE A QUIET SPIRIT

*A constant serenity arising from within,
as I trust that God controls every detail of my life.*

**"Your adornment must not be merely external—
braiding the hair, and wearing gold jewelry,
or putting on dresses; but let it be the hidden
person of the heart, with the imperishable
quality of a gentle and quiet spirit,
which is precious in the sight of God."
I Peter 3:3, 4**

Prayer Points:

"Your adornment must not be merely external—braiding the hair, and wearing gold jewelry, or putting on dresses; but let it be the hidden person of the heart, with the imperishable quality of a gentle and quiet spirit, which is precious in the sight of God. "
I Peter 3:3, 4

When a beautiful woman is portrayed in contemporary culture, the visible outer appearance is the focal point of attractiveness. External physical attributes and personal adornment, such as clothing, makeup, jewelry and hairstyles, constitute notions of beauty. Man looks on the outward appearance but God looks on the heart (I Samuel 16:7).

While not condemning physical attractiveness, the Lord does say in 1 Peter 3 that we women should take special care to adorn ourselves with true beauty; the inner person, the hidden person of our heart.

The adornment of a quiet spirit is something that God considers to be of precious value. Unlike clothes, or physical attractiveness, a quiet spirit is a quality that will not perish. A woman may be born physically beautiful through no effort of her own, but true inner beauty is something with which every woman has the volition of adorning herself.

Someone once said, "It's not a woman's fault if she is not beautiful at sixteen, but it is if she is not beautiful at sixty." True inner beauty should increase with time and maturity.

A gentle and quiet spirit truly makes a woman beautiful. Unfortunately, the concept of quietness is easily misunderstood. Some women erroneously assume that having a quiet spirit implies wearing only gray clothing, sitting in the back of a room, and never speaking. This is not at all what constitutes a quiet spirit.

Quiet does not simply mean "silent and dull." **Webster's New World College Dictionary** defines "quiet" this way:

    a)   *still; calm; motionless*
    b)   *not making noise; hushed (a quiet motor); not speaking, silent.*
    c)   *not agitated as in motion; gentle (a quiet sea)*
    d)   *not easily excited or disturbed (a quiet disposition)*
    e)   *not ostentatious or pretentious (quiet furnishings)*
    f)   *not forward; unobtrusive (a quiet manner)*

g) *secluded (a quiet den)*
h) *peaceful and relaxing (a quiet evening at home)*
i) *in commerce, not busy (a quiet day on the stock exchange)*

Scripture uses a variety of words in the Hebrew and Greek to capture what we would translate today as "quiet." The biblical definition of all of them can be summed up as meaning "tranquil."

There are two basic thrusts to the word "quiet" in Scripture. The first usage of the word connotes "tranquility arising from without." It has to do with calm circumstances that are conducive to peacefulness. Examples of this usage are found in describing the "quiet life" of societal peace (I Timothy 2:2), the absence of war yielding "peace and quiet" (I Chronicles 22:9), and in the elements of nature, such as the sea being "quiet" (Jeremiah 49:23).

The second usage of words translated "quiet" implies "tranquility arising from within, causing no disturbance to others." The prime example of this usage is found in 1 Peter 3 where women are exhorted to adorn themselves with a gentle and quiet spirit.

The "quiet spirit" which is precious in the sight of the Lord is a tranquility arising from within. Even though external conditions may not foster peacefulness, a quiet spirit is one that is calm, not anxious, and doesn't worry. A quiet spirit is unflappable and is not easily agitated or disturbed by daily cares or uncomfortable circumstances

1. How would you rate yourself on exhibiting a quiet spirit?

    a) On the line on the next page, circle the number which best depicts where you would rate the degree of your own quiet spirit.

    b) Put an "H" in the area where your husband would probably place your display of a quiet spirit. If you are single, indicate where your parents might rate your quiet spirit.

    c) Put an "X" in the area where your children would probably place your display of a quiet spirit. If you are single, indicate where your siblings, or roommates, might rate your quiet spirit.

(You might ask your family members to actually "rate" your quiet spirit. If so, remember that we tend to see how far we've come, while others tend to see how far we have to go. Don't be discouraged!)

Prayer Points:

0	1	2	3	4	5	6	7	8	9	10

easily irritated   unruffled

worried   content

restless   calm

2. What is it that tends to cause you to worry, to be anxious, or "gets you in a dither?" Take a moment and write down anything that comes to mind regarding things, events, or people that disturb your sense of inner peace.

    a)

    b)

    c)

As you look at your responses above, do you see any areas that are linked to fear? Fear disturbs a quiet spirit. When we allow fear to take a foothold in our hearts and minds, our spirit is instantly disquieted.

Scripture links a quiet spirit with a lack of fear.

Proverbs 1:33 "But he who listens to me shall live securely And will be at ease from the dread of evil."

Jeremiah 30:10 "'Fear not, O Jacob My servant,' declares the LORD, 'And do not be dismayed, O Israel; For behold, I will save you from afar and your offspring from the land of their captivity. And Jacob will return and will be quiet and at ease, And no one will make him afraid.'"

Jeremiah 49:23 "For they have heard bad news; They are disheartened. There is anxiety by the sea, It cannot be calmed."

I Peter 3:4-6 "... but let it be the hidden person of the heart, with the imperishable quality of a gentle and quiet spirit, which is precious in the sight of God. For in this way in former times the holy women also, who hoped in God, used to adorn themselves, being submissive to their own husbands; just as Sarah obeyed Abraham, calling him lord, and you have become her children if you do what is right without being frightened by any fear."

Worry has been defined as "a trickle of fear that meanders through the mind cutting a channel into which all other thoughts are drained." Worry is a by-product of fear.

Perhaps our quiet spirit is ruffled by fears regarding our health, our relationships with others, our husband, job security, evil that could harm those whom we love, finances, or unknowns regarding the future. Many of us have encountered that disquieted spirit in the wee hours of the morning when "molehills become mountains" in our minds.

We all know women who seem to enjoy worrying. To nurture and feed on worry or fear is wrong. It is sin, and it leads to more sin. Psalm 37:8 tells us:

"do not fret, it leads only to evildoing."

3.   We know that God has not given us a spirit of fear (II Timothy 1:7). The Lord refers to fear as a spiritual issue. If He has not given us this fear, from where do you think fear may originate?

What is the antidote for disquieting fears? God never tells us to do something without making it possible for us. Deuteronomy 30:11 tells us that God's command

"is not too difficult for you, nor is it out of reach."

So how do we reclaim that quiet spirit?

It may not be instantaneous. We see in the book of Job that adorning ourselves with a quiet spirit is often a process that takes time. As we mature in the Lord, however, we should see the Holy Spirit giving us increasing victory as we seek that inner peace which God loves to see in us.

The first step involved in nurturing a quiet spirit is to recognize Who God is. What do the following verses reveal about His nature?

GOD ALONE IS IN CONTROL. HE IS SOVEREIGN:

4.   Psalm 46:10

5.   Isaiah 14:24, 27

6.   Psalm 31:15

7.   Psalm 139:16

How might knowing that God is actively controlling every detail of your life help you to nurture a quiet spirit?

GOD REMEMBERS AND CARES:

8.   Isaiah 49:14-16

9.   Psalm 56:8

10.   Matthew 10:29-31

How might understanding that God is deeply involved and concerned about every detail of your life help you to nurture a quiet spirit?

GOD IS GOOD:

11.   Lamentations 3:31-33

12.   Jeremiah 29:11

13.   Romans 8:28

How might knowing that God always does what is best in your life help you to nurture a quiet spirit?

God's Word tells us how to combat disquieting thoughts and attitudes. Adorning ourselves with a quiet spirit is a spiritual issue. Giving ourselves pep talks on "positive thinking" is not the answer. We cannot do it in our own strength; we need the power of the indwelling Holy Spirit to change us. We must saturate our mind with God's Word (Psalm 119:165). We are to be continually being transformed by the renewing of our minds in Christ (Romans 12:2).

14.   In Philippians 4:6, what is the command given to us?

        What should be our attitude toward God?

When any anxious thought enters our heart or mind, we have a choice to make. We can allow that anxiety to multiply (Psalm 94:19), or we can take it to Jesus in prayer and leave it with Him. The choice is clear, and the results are evident:

Prayer Points:

"Being anxious" leads to evil doing (Psalm 37:8);

"Praying" leads us into God's holy presence (Hebrews 4:16).

"Being anxious" focuses on tomorrow's "maybes" (James 5:13–15);

"Praying" focuses on tomorrow's "truth" (John 14:6).

"Being anxious" robs us of enjoying "today" (Matthew 6:33);

"Praying" frees us to be about God's business "today" (Psalm 139:16).

"Being anxious" focuses on ourselves and our circumstances (Matthew 14:30);

"Praying" turns our attention on Jesus and His power (Matthew 14:28, 29).

"Being anxious" weighs us down in exhaustion and fatigue (Psalm 38:4–8);

"Praying" relieves our weariness as "Another" carries our burden (I Peter 5:7).

"Being anxious" doesn't accomplish "anything" (Matthew 6:27);

"Praying" cooperates with God to accomplish "everything" (Ephesians 3:20).

"Being anxious" results in personal frustration (Matthew 6:27);

"Praying" builds confidence and trust in the Lord (Philippians 1:6).

"Being anxious" is a sin (Philippians 4:6);

"Praying" delights the Lord (Proverbs 15:8).

"Being anxious" sucks "contentment" out of our lives;

"Praying" is a prerequisite to "learning to be content" (Philippians 4:6, 7).

"Being anxious" leads to hopeless despair (Psalm 42:5);

"Praying" results in experiencing the peace of God (Philippians 4:7).

15.   In Philippians 4:7, what does God promise to do when we bring our requests to Him?

Have you ever prayed about something only to have your worries return?

16.   In Philippians 4:8, when we pray about issues of concern or worry, we give those anxious thoughts to the Lord. Yet, we cannot stop there. We must practice mental discipline and begin to actually control those things on which our minds dwell. This verse lists eight adjectives that specifically describe what we should be thinking about. List these chronologically in the spaces below.

Think about these things....   Definition

a. _____ *That which is in accordance with reality as God sees it*

b. _____ *That which is dignified, upright, and untarnished*

c. _____ *That which is according to what is just, good or proper*

d. _____ *That which is spotless and untainted; without any impurity*

e. _____ *That which is delightful and beloved*

f. _____ *That which has a good reputation and is admirable*

g. _____ *That which is superior, above the norm, and virtuous*

h. _____ *That which qualifies for commendation and would elicit applause*

As you consider specific nagging thoughts that tend to disrupt your quiet spirit, would you say that those thoughts, or worries, would meet the above criterion? Put a checkmark beside any of the above "thought patterns" that you may be neglecting.

The struggle to adorn ourselves with a quiet spirit is fought in the battlefield of our mind.

17.   Isaiah 26:3, 4 What is the secret to experiencing "perfect peace"?

Prayer Points:

18.   II Corinthians 10:3-5 What are we to do with our thoughts?

We must capture and inspect each incoming idea that seeks entry into our mind. As Kay Arthur suggests, we need to do the "Philippians Frisk." We must scrutinize each thought by asking; "Are you true? Are you honorable, right, pure, and lovely? Are you admirable, excellent, and praiseworthy?" Any thought that fails any one of these eight levels of inspection must be subjugated and not allowed entrance into our thought-life.

We must learn to "harness our hearts" and to "frisk our thoughts" in order to experience that quiet spirit that God longs to see in us. Yet, rather than merely focusing on pushing away "bad" thoughts, we need to replace those unholy ideas with God's "good" ideas. In order to maintain a quiet spirit, it is imperative that we intentionally "dwell on these things" that Paul lists in Philippians 4:8.

Paul tells us in Philippians that the Lord will work in us throughout our entire lives to make us like Christ (1:6; 2:13; 3:12-14), yet he also tells us that we have the responsibility to "practice" mental discipline (4:9).

19.   II Timothy 1:7   What three things has God given us to provide victory over fear?

Optional: Look up the words "power," "love" and "discipline" in your concordance or expository dictionary. (The King James Version translates "discipline" as "sound mind.") How might these three things work to provide victory over fear?

20.   Psalm 131:2   King David occasionally succumbed to a
        disquieted spirit (Psalm 42:5). What steps did he take to
        regain a quiet spirit?

        What do you think that David meant when he described his
        rest as being like that of a weaned child as opposed to a
        nursing child?

We see that training ourselves to develop a quiet spirit, and adorning
ourselves with it, is a choice that we make; a choice involving personal
discipline and responsibility.

As women desiring to be seen by God as having true inner beauty, we
must make a decision to be obedient in this area of our lives. Relying
on the Holy Spirit to empower us to discipline ourselves in this area, we
must take steps to begin adorning ourselves with the quiet spirit that
God sees as precious.

21.   What is it that you need to eliminate this week from your life in
        order to have the quality of a quiet spirit?

22.   What is it that you need to begin doing in your life this week to
        increase that quality of a quiet spirit?

Prayer Points:

SUMMARY:

Define "having a quiet spirit" in your own terms. You could use a synonym, a motto, a poem or prayer, or even make a drawing to show your understanding of this character trait.

DISCUSSION:

Isaiah 30:15 reads, "For thus the LORD God, the Holy One of Israel, has said, 'In repentance and rest you shall be saved, in quietness and trust is your strength.'"

What do you think that this means?

APPLICATION:

For married women:
A neighbor confides in you that she can't seem to stop being fearful and worried about her children. Though her school-aged children are quite responsible, she won't even allow them to play in the front yard. She says that she would like to stop being such a nervous wreck, but feels that there's nothing she can do about it. How would you counsel this neighbor?

For single women:
Another single woman in your workplace confides to you that she is exhausted because she has recently been losing sleep. It seems that every night she is plagued with fearful thoughts that lead her to worry about the future. How would you counsel this coworker?

CHAPTER SIX

Be Dignified

*Possessing a seriousness of purpose in life
which is evident in my conduct*

**"Strength and dignity are her clothing,
And she smiles at the future. "
Proverbs 31:25**

**"Strength and dignity are her clothing,
And she smiles at the future. "
Proverbs 31:25**

Prayer Points:

What comes to mind when you think of a dignified woman?

Some may picture a humorless aristocratic woman with a fetish for "high tea." Others may envision a snooty woman wearing conservative clothing. Does the word "dignified" leave a good taste in your mouth? Describe your image of a dignified woman.

We can assume that the quality of being dignified is very desirable because the Lord instructs men of all ages to be dignified (Titus 2:2,7,8), and also deacons and their wives to be dignified (I Timothy 3:11).

The excellent woman that we find in Proverbs 31 is also clothed in dignity (Proverbs 31:25).

Being dignified is a mark of Christian maturity, which is a trait that the Lord loves to see in women.

Webster's New World College Dictionary defines 'dignity' this way:

a) *the quality of being worthy of esteem or honor; worthiness*
b) *high repute; honor.*
c) *the degree of worth, repute or honor.*
d) *a high position, rank, or title.*
e) *a dignitary.*
f) *loftiness of appearance or manner; stateliness.*
g) *proper pride and self-respect.*

We find the concept of "dignity" in both the New and the Old Testaments. The New Testament term for dignity, ("semnos"), is also translated as meaning "grave," or "serious," in some translations of Scripture. Dignity, as used in the New Testament text, points to the quality of one possessing a seriousness of purpose. The term also connotes self respect which is evident in one's conduct.

The Old Testament term for dignity, ("hadar"), is manifested by the honor and splendor surrounding God Himself (I Chronicles 16:27; Psalm 104:1), God's sanctuary (Psalm 96:6), and God's creation. It stresses the worthiness and splendor surrounding one's personal presence.

In order to grasp the significance of "dignity" as used in Scripture, we must combine both the New Testament and Old Testament concepts of the term. The picture of a dignified woman is not "one dimensional." The composite picture of dignity painted by the Lord in Scripture is "three dimensional."

A woman of dignity is distinguished by these three things:

I.   Having a proper view of "self"-respect.

II.   Possessing a seriousness of purpose in life.

III.   Radiating honor and splendor from her personal presence.

What does God's Word reveal regarding these three ingredients which comprise dignity?

I.   HAVE A PROPER VIEW OF "SELF"-RESPECT

As modern influences have tended to dehumanize human beings and make them feel worthless, Satan has capitalized on this. He has instigated a counterfeit sense of self worth. The New Age concept of human potential being virtually limitless is dangerously leading many women astray from a true perspective on human dignity.

What is a proper view of "self" in light of God's Word? How do we see ourselves accurately? This is an area where there is a great spiritual battle. Satan desires to confuse this issue in the minds and hearts of contemporary women.

There are two extreme, unbiblical views of self that are both detrimental to being women of dignity. One extreme perspective is that we are worthless and of no value whatsoever. Some women question how God could value them enough to send Jesus to die for them. Many have difficulty reconciling these to two truths:

**Prayer
Points:**

1) Though their fallen, sinful self is unworthy of salvation,

2) God has ascribed great worth to them and His Son personally died for them.

Some women find it difficult to comprehend that they are of incredibly immense value to God; that they are precious to Him.

Satan has used this misconception to keep women from believing that God loves them. Spiritual warfare erupts when we listen to Satan whispering that God could not value us enough to send His Son to save us.

God's Word tells us the truth. We cannot rely on feelings to validate the truth. It is a fact that God loves us individually and places great value in us.

We must remember that just as parents give children gifts which are unearned and undeserved, God gives us the gift of salvation which is unearned and undeserved. Much like that gift-giving parent, the Father derives intense joy from providing for His child.

William Temple said, "My worth is what I am worth to God, and that is a marvelous great deal because Christ died for me." Jesus came to give His life as a ransom for many (Mark 10:45).

How should we view ourselves in light of God's Word?

1.   Psalm 40:5

2.   Psalm 139:13, 14

3.   Psalm 8:3-6

4.   Ephesians 1:4

We are extremely valuable to God. Unlike any other creation, God created us in His own image (Genesis 1:26) and called it "very good" (1:31). He loves you so much that He sent His only Son to die for you. Yes, you, personally.

God calls us His "treasured ones" (Psalm 83:3), and David tells us that "As for the saints who are in the earth, They are the majestic ones in whom is all my delight." (Psalm 16:3). If our Creator treasures us so much, then we are wrong not to acknowledge and appreciate how He values us.

The moment that we being to recognize God's great love for us, and the value that He places on each of our lives, is the time when we begin to become "dignified women."

A second erroneous perspective of "self" being touted in contemporary society is that man is indeed quite worthy by nature. Our self-absorbed culture portrays man as having natural, unlimited potential. Humanity is presented as being quasi-divine, and innately worthy of highest praise.

Popular music instructs that the act of loving yourself is "the greatest love of all." We are constantly being bombarded with exhortations to "love ourselves." Yet, is this an accurate view of "self" from God's perspective? What does Scripture say?

5.   II Timothy 3:1-4

        What is the first symptom given of the difficult times
        that will occur in the last days?

        Who are men choosing not to love?

6.   Luke 10:27 (also read Ephesians 5:29)

        Is this a command to love ourselves? Why or why not?

7.   Romans 12:3. What warning is given here?

Prayer Points:

Dignity in the Christian life requires a proper view of "self"-respect. There must be a balance between self-denial and self-affirmation. Scripture is clear that, on one hand, it is vanity to think too highly of ourselves, and, on the other hand, it is sin (and tragic) to underestimate or misunderstand the value and love that God has for each of us.

How do we resolve this apparent contradiction, and develop a biblically accurate self-view?

The cross of Jesus Christ supplies the answer and the divine example. At the cross, Christ resolves the issue by His demonstration of both SELF-DENIAL (He did not claim His heavenly rights), and SELF-AFFIRMATION (He knew Who He was, and what the Father was accomplishing through His obedience).

How is self-denial discussed in the following verses?

8.   Mark 8:34

9.   Galatians 5:24

10.   Romans 12:1, 2

The "self" that we are to deny, disown, and crucify, is our fallen self. Everything within us that is hostile toward and incompatible with Jesus Christ must be repudiated. We must deny anything about us that is the result of our sin nature.

The "self" that we are to respect, affirm, and value, is that part of us that God originally created man to be. We must respect and affirm the fact that we were created in the image of God (Genesis 1:26, 27). As dignified women, maintaining a proper view of "self"-respect will always impact our personal conduct. We will avoid disgraceful activities and focus on things that are proper and fitting (Ephesians 5:3, 4, 11, 12).

When we accurately see ourselves as God sees us, we will be quick to acknowledge and repent from sin, and we will yearn to experience intimacy with Him.

II.   POSSESS A SERIOUSNESS OF PURPOSE IN LIFE

We were created by God for a specific and unique purpose. True dignity is living with such intensity as to reflect the seriousness of fulfilling that purpose in a devout way.

King David served the purpose of God in his own generation (Acts 13:36). Esther realized that the circumstances of her life were designed for specific purposes (Esther 4:14).

What do the following Scriptures reveal about God's special design for each of us?

11.   Isaiah 64:8

12.   Romans 9:20, 21

13.   Ephesians 2:10

Prayer Points:

Prayer Points:

Optional: Look up the meaning of the Greek term "workmanship" as found in Ephesians 2:10. How does this "word-picture" demonstrate God's unique plan for your life?

Each individual has been uniquely created by God for specific purposes. A dignified woman understands that her Creator has placed her on earth, at a precise time, to accomplish certain things. She has a sense of destiny. A sense of seriousness permeates the life of a dignified woman as she seeks to fulfill God's will and purpose for her life.

III.   RADIATE HONOR AND SPLENDOR FROM ONE'S PERSONAL PRESENCE

The world tells us that dignity and honor result from external circumstances of life. What does Scripture tell us about honor that comes from the following?

14.   Physical appearance - I Samuel 16:7

15.   Others' opinions - Proverbs 29:25

16.   Wealth - Matthew 6:19-21

17.   Social status - James 2:2-8; II Corinthians 10:12, 18

The concept of nobility is found both in contemporary dictionary definitions of "dignified" as well as in the biblical definition. Though none of us may have attained nobility through natural birth or through marriage, what nobility do we possess as Christian women?

18.   II Corinthians 6:18

19.   Galatians 4:4-7

What term is used to describe Jesus Christ?

What was His purpose in dying on the cross?

What evidence do believing women have of being His daughters?

What else accompanies being His son or daughter?

20.   Romans 8:14-17

What accompanies being His child?

What legal process accomplished our status of nobility?

Prayer Points:

Nothing could be more noble than being related to the King of kings (I Timothy 6:15). As daughters of the Father, we become legitimate princesses; as the bride of the returning King of kings (Revelation 19:16), we find ourselves in incredible, incomparable nobility. We truly have reason to conduct ourselves as believers with absolute dignity.

Look up the following references where the Aramaic word for dignity ("hadar") is used.

21.   Psalm 104:1, 2

Who is being described?

How is His honor displayed?

22.   Proverbs 31:25

Who is being described?

How is her honor displayed?

It is no accident that the Scriptures use the same word to describe the way that the Father displays His dignity and the way that an excellent wife displays her dignity. Our Lord desires that we be like Himself in the way that we live (I Peter 1:16).

Throughout Scripture, when an individual entered into the presence of the Lord, God's splendor and majesty were unavoidably noticeable. The Lord's "dignity" always impacted those around Him. Those entering into His presence sensed His holiness (Exodus 3:5), and being in the presence of God made individuals keenly aware of their own personal sin (Isaiah 6:5-7).

As women created in the image of God, filled with the indwelling Holy

Spirit, our presence should likewise be noticeable to those around us. Others should respond to Christ in us. Our conduct should build others up and urge them on toward godliness.

We are to be women of dignity. Take a moment and evaluate your own life in light of today's study. How well are you doing in exhibiting the following aspects of being dignified?

Prayer Points:

Are self-respect and a sense of personal value to God evident in my conduct?

Does my life exhibit seriousness of purpose?

Would others say that my life radiates an "honor and splendor?"

Would others notice that I am a Christian?

What changes need to be made in my attitudes or actions?

Prayer Points:

SUMMARY:

Define "being dignified" in your own terms. You could use a synonym, a motto, a poem or prayer, or even make a drawing to show your understanding of this character trait.

DISCUSSION:

Scripture speaks of women being "clothed" in dignity (Proverbs 31:25). How does one go about doing this?

APPLICATION:

The local public school is teaching building self-esteem to the student body. Some of the Christians whom you know are questioning whether or not this teaching is biblical. What do you think about this situation?

CHAPTER SEVEN

Be Reverent in Behavior

Living in a sacred way that is

suitable as a child of God.

**"Older women likewise are to be reverent
in their behavior..."
Titus 2:3**

"Older women likewise are to be reverent in their behavior…"
Titus 2:3

Prayer Points:

A faith that does not impact our actions is a dead faith (James 2:17). Living faith manifests itself both in a changed inner life, and in changed external behavior. Women who love the Lord exemplify the characteristic of being "reverent in behavior."

Webster's New World College Dictionary defines "reverent" as:

Feeling, showing, or characterized by reverence.

"Reverence" is defined as:

a) *a feeling or attitude of deep respect, love and awe, as for something sacred; veneration*

b) *a manifestation of this; specif., a bow, curtsy, or similar gesture of respect, obeisance. The state of being revered*

Titus 2:3, where older women are exhorted to "be reverent in behavior," is the only place in Scripture where the term is used. One Greek word, "hieroprepos," captures the content of the entire English phrase. "Hieroprepos" is actually a combination of two separate Greek words:

a) "hieros" - meaning sacred or holy, especially used in regard to God's temple, suited to sacred character.

b) "prepo" - to be fitting, clearly seen.

It is God's desire that women conduct themselves with such a sacred demeanor that their actions would be appropriate and suitable for serving in His holy temple.

> ***Optional:** Using your concordance and Bible dictionary, look up "temple" or "tabernacle" in the Scriptures. What types of descriptions, restrictions, and regulations are found regarding this place?

It is quite evident from God's Word that He has high demands and expectations regarding His temple.

What do the following verses reveal about God's temple?

**Prayer
Points:**

1.   Psalm 93:5

        What does the Lord expect in His temple?

2.   I Corinthians 3:16, 17

The temple in Jerusalem was where God's presence dwelt in the Holy of Holies. This temple was destroyed in 70 A.D. by the Romans. According to these verses, where is the temple today?

        Where does His Holy Spirit now dwell?

3.   I Corinthians 6:19, 20

        Why are we to glorify God in our bodies?

        How do you think that you could glorify God in your
        body? (It may be helpful to read the preceding verses 12-18.)

4.   II Corinthians 6:14-16

        What two types of people are contrasted?

        Which type is the temple of the living God?

Which type are you?

**Prayer
Points:**

What does that make you?

God "has saved us and called us with a holy calling, not according to our works, but according to His own purpose and grace..." (II Timothy 1:9). Our bodies are a temple of God and He has called us to holiness.

5.   I Peter 1:15, 16; Leviticus 11:44a, 20:26
       What does God expect of us?

6.   Romans 12:1   (The strong use of the Greek word "urge" here
       implies to "twist-your-arm.")

Holiness means "set apart to God." When we are saved we become holy to God. Just as we are saved through no merit of our own (Ephesians 2:8, 9), we also live a godly life not in our own strength. It is through the empowering of the indwelling Holy Spirit that believers are enabled to live in a way that is pleasing to Him.

What do the following verses tell us about holy, godly living?

7.   Titus 2:11, 12

       What is it that instructs us in godly living?

8.   Romans 8:13

       What do spiritual women do?

9.   Galatians 5:19-25

        What are the deeds of the flesh?

        What is the fruit of the Spirit?

        Which of these two lists most typifies your behavior?

Our bodies are the temple of God. We are called to godliness which is suitable for God's holy temple. We are to put the deeds of the flesh to death. How are you doing at presenting your body as a living and holy sacrifice?

Let's "examine ourselves" (II Corinthians 13:5) and look specifically at some of our "spiritual physiology." What do the following Scriptures tell us about our:

EYES:

10.   Psalm 101:3

        What things in your life are "worthless things?"

11.   Matthew 5:27-30

Prayer Points:

12.   Job 31:1

What did Job do about his "eye problem?"

EARS:

13.   Isaiah 33:15, 16

Do you enjoy hearing media accounts of violent crimes or famous murders?

14.   Psalm 101:7

TONGUES:

15.   Ephesians 4:29

16.   Proverbs 30:32

17.   II Timothy 2:16

HANDS:

18.   Ephesians 4:28

    If undercharged at a store, do you return the money?

    Do you physically work hard?

    Are you quick to share the fruits of your labors?

19.   Psalm 18:20

FEET:

20.   Psalm 1:1

21.   II Timothy 2:22

    Do you physically avoid people, places, or things which arouse
    wrong desires in you? Give an example.

Prayer Points:

Is there any area in which your body is not behaving in a way that is suitable and fitting for the holy temple of God? Note any area in which the Holy Spirit may have prodded you in the above Scriptures to present your body as a holy and living sacrifice to God.

22.   Romans 6:12, 13

How do the members of our body become instruments of righteousness?

Someone once said that the only problem with a "living" sacrifice is that it keeps crawling off of the altar. When we do fall, we are to immediately confess it as sin and place ourselves back up on that altar (I John 1:9). God still loves us; He will never leave us or forsake us (Hebrews 13:5).

23.   Romans 8:38, 39

What can separate us from the love of God?

24.   I John 2:1

What does John say about sin?

Is he writing to believers or to unbelievers?

Reverent behavior is not limited to that which we might consider to be "religious" by nature. It is deadly and dangerous to compartmentalize our Christian lives by segmenting "Christian activities" from "everyday life." To the Lord, everything that we do is a spiritual act. All of our behavior should be reverent. This is pointed out clearly in Colossians 3:23, 24.

"Whatever may be your task, work at it heartily (from the soul), as something done for the Lord and not for men, knowing (with all certainty) that it is from the Lord, and not from men, that you will receive the inheritance which is your (real) reward. (The One Whom) you are actually serving is the Lord Christ, the Messiah."
(The Amplified Bible)

25.   What is your "work" in life? List the main things that dominate your time and your energies.

a)

b)

c)

d)

e)

Do you sense when you are doing these activities that you are doing them as a sacred act of worship for the Lord?

26.   Scripture exhorts us to "discipline yourself for the purpose of godliness" (1 Timothy 4:7). What things could you change in your attitudes and actions that would increase the reverent nature of your behavior?

What will you do this week to begin making those changes?

Prayer Points:

SUMMARY:

Define "reverent in behavior" in your own terms. You could use a synonym, a motto, a poem or prayer, or even make a drawing to show your understand of this character trait.

DISCUSSION:

How would you recognize a woman who is reverent in behavior?

APPLICATION:

A church friend comes to you for help. She confides that she has a habit of serious sin that she has been unable to break all of her life. She is wondering if she is going to go to hell because of this sin. What counsel do you give to her?

The moment that we receive Jesus Christ as our personal Savior we begin the great adventure of "walking with the Lord."

Life truly is a journey. Each decision that we make will either take us away from the path that God has for our lives, or it will take us deeper into the heart and will of our Lord. With each step that we take along the pathway of obedience, we will experience Jesus' presence more intimately (John 14:21). The Lord has laid out "ancient paths" in Scripture that will lead us in "the good way" where we will "find rest for our souls" (Jeremiah 6:16). When we follow these ancient paths, we will experience fullness of joy and pleasures forever (Psalm 16:11). Through His Word, God teaches us "everything pertaining to life and godliness" (II Peter 1:3).

Now that you have completed, and applied, the biblical principles from this Ancient Paths I Bible study to your life, you have begun making progress along the Lord's road for your life. In Ancient Paths II, III, and IV, we will continue our journey with Him as He leads us walking in our marriages, homes, churches, and communities. His Word is practical, direct, and applicable to our lives today.

Christ is the One who began the good work in your life and He will complete it (Philippians 1:6; 2:13). The Lord has much more in store for your life (Jeremiah 29:11). Keep moving ahead (Philippians 3:13, 14)! Continue to pursue the Lord and follow Him with a whole heart.

> **"As you therefore have received Christ Jesus the Lord,**
> **so walk in Him."**
> **Colossians 2:6**

Prayer Points:

Recommended Reading
References and Resources

Chapter 1.
> "The Road Not Taken" from The Poetry of Robert Frost. 1969, by Henry Holt and Company.
> Salvation, Lewis Sperry Chafer, Dunham Publishing Company, 1917.

Chapter 3.
> The Practice of Godliness, Jerry Bridges, Navpress, 1986.
> The God You Can Know, Dan DeHaan, Moody Press, 1982.
> Knowing God, J.I. Packer, Intervarsity Press, 1993.

Chapter 4.
> The Measure of a Woman, Gene A. Getz, Regal Books, 1977.

Chapter 5.
> Keep a Quiet Heart, Elisabeth Elliot, Servant Publications, 1995
> The Christian's Secret of a Happy Life, Hannah Whithall Smith,, Fleming Revell, 1952.

Chapter 6.
> Self Confrontation Manual, John C. Broger, Biblical Counseling Foundation, 1991.

Chapter 7.
> "A Call to Holiness," (video), Nancy Leigh DeMoss, Life Action Ministries, 2003.
> The Heart God Purifies, Nancy Leigh DeMoss, Moody Press, 2002.
> The Practice of the Presence of GOD, Brother Lawrence, Whitaker House, 1982.

Unless otherwise noted, all Bible quotations used in this study are taken from the New American Standard Bible. The Lockman Foundation

Holy Bible: New International Version. Copyright 1978 by the New York International Bible Society

Webster's New World College Dictionary, Third Edition, Simon & Schuster, Inc., 1997.

How to Do the *Optional Word Studies

The *Optional* word studies from each chapter are designed to enhance your understanding of each week's lesson. In order to do these *Optional* studies you will need access to some books that will broaden your ability to study the Bible for yourself.

There are two basic approaches recommended for doing your word studies.

1.   *The first approach requires two study resource books:*

·   Strong's Exhaustive Concordance of the Bible; James Strong, S.T.D., LL.D.; MacDonald Publishing Company, McLean, Virginia, 22102.

·   Vine's Complete Expository Dictionary of Old and New Testament Words; W. E. Vine, Merrill F. Unger, William White, Jr.; Copyright 1985 by Thomas Nelson Publishers.

An exhaustive concordance is a book containing every word of the text of the Bible, and every occurrence of each word in sequential order. It is important to use a concordance that is compatible with the translation version of Scripture that you are using.

Concordance words are arranged alphabetically by topic. Underneath the highlighted word that you are studying, you will find the abbreviated Bible references, in sequential order, of every place where that word is located in Scripture. Printed to the right of each reference is the text where that word is used in the Bible. To the far right of the printed text you will see a code number.

In the back of your concordance are located two dictionaries; the Old Testament dictionary is in Hebrew, and the New Testament Dictionary is in Greek. Look up the code number in the appropriate dictionary, and you will find the exact word used in the original language, along with the definition of that word.

If you would like more in-depth study of the original meaning of that word, you may use a Vine's Expository Dictionary of Old and New Testament Words. The Expository Dictionary is organized alphabetically in English, and amplifies the abbreviated definition that you will find in the back of your concordance. The code numbers located in Vine's are the same as Strong's Concordance numbers.

**2.	*The second approach requires three study resource books:***

·	The Complete Word Study New Testament; Spiros Zodhiates, Th.D.; Copyright 1991 by AMG International, Inc. Publishers, Chattanooga, TN, 37422

If you would like more in-depth study of the original meaning of that word, you may use:

·	The Complete Word Study Old Testament; Spiros Zodhiates, Th.D.; Copyright 1994 by AMG International, Inc. D/B/A AMG Publishers, Chattanooga, TN, 37422

·	The Complete Word Study Dictionary New Testament; Spiros Zodhiates, Th.D.; Copyright 1992 by AMG International, Inc. Publishers, Chattanooga, TN,

The Complete Word Study New and Old Testaments contain the entire Biblical texts in the King James Version. As you read the text, you will find a code number above each word. The Word Study Testaments use a numbering system that is compatible with both Vine's Expository Dictionary and Strong's Exhaustive Concordance. These numbers are all interchangeable. Look up that number in the dictionary located in the back of your Word Study Testament. There you will find the precise meaning of the word as used in the original language.

If you want further elaboration of the meaning of a New Testament word, you can use The Complete Word Study Dictionary New Testament. At this time, a Word Study Dictionary of the Old Testament has not yet been published. This New Testament dictionary is organized numerically, rather than topically, in English. Look up your code number in the dictionary to find a more in-depth definition of the word that you are studying.

Glossary

- **Called** – designated, invited, set apart by an action of God to some spiritual sphere and manner of being

- **Confession** – to agree with God by openly admitting personal guilt regarding that of which one is accused

- **Faith** – believing obedience; taking a promise at face value, trusting in the pledge of a person that results in responsive action

- **Flesh** – the unregenerate state of men; the weaker element in human nature

- **Glorification** – to be magnified, extolled and praised

- **Glory** – to ascribe honor to; to praise

- **Godliness** – having a heart for God that manifests itself by living in such a way that is well-pleasing to the Lord

- **Gospel** – the good news

- **Grace** – God's unmerited favor and gifts to humanity

- **Holiness** – set apart and dedicated to God; pure, devoted

- **Justification** – to be declared or pronounced righteous; acquittal

- **Law** – God's commandments to Israel; Mosaic Law

- **Peace** – wholeness and well-being in all relationships

- **Propitiation** – the merciful means whereby God covers and passes over man's sin, atonement

- **Redemption** – to purchase with a view toward one's freedom; to release on receipt of ransom

- **Repentance** – a change of mind about something that one has been doing wrongly, coupled with a resolve to begin doing the right thing

- **Righteousness** – the state of being in the right, or declared to be "not guilty"

- **Saints** – all those who have been set apart, holy, dedicated to God

- Salvation – spiritual and eternal deliverance given immediately by God to those who accept His conditions of repentance and faith in Jesus Christ His Son

- Sanctification – separated to God; resulting in a believer's separation from evil things and evil ways, and his being empowered to realize the will of God in his life

- Sin – "missing the mark", disobedience to Divine law

- Soul – the breath of life; the immaterial, invisible part of man; the natural life of the body including perception, feelings, intellect, personality and desires

- Sovereign – above and superior to all; supreme in power, rank, and authority; holding the position of ruler; royalty

- Spirit – the life principle bestowed on man by God; an element similar to, but higher than the soul, affecting both the soul and the body

- Wrath – God's righteous response to evil, His refusal to condone unrighteousness and His judgment upon it

Becoming a Follower of Christ

1. Recognize that God loves you:

"For God so loved the world that He gave His one and only Son, that whoever believes in Him shall not perish but have eternal life." (John 3:16)

"But God demonstrates His own love for us in this: While we were still sinners, Christ died for us." (Romans 5:8)

2. Admit that you are a sinner:

"For all have sinned and fall short of the glory of God." (Romans 3:23)

"As it is written: 'There is no one righteous, not even one.'" (Romans 3:10)

3. Recognize Jesus Christ as being God's only remedy for sin:

"For the wages of sin is death, but the gift of God is eternal life in Christ Jesus our Lord." (Romans 6:23)

"Yet all who received Him, to those who believed in His name, He gave the right to become children of God." (John 1:12)

"For what I received I passed on to you as of first importance: that Christ died for our sins according to the Scriptures, that He was buried, that He was raised on the third day according to the Scriptures." (I Corinthians 15:3, 4)

4. Receive Jesus Christ as your personal Savior:

"If you confess with your mouth, 'Jesus is Lord,' and believe in your heart that God raised Him from the dead, you will be saved." (Romans 10:9)

Prayer is simply "talking with God." Right now, go to God in prayer and ask Christ to be your Savior. You might pray something like this:

"Lord Jesus, I need You. I confess that I am a sinner and that You paid the penalty for my sin through Your death on the cross. I believe that You died for my sins and were raised from the dead. I ask You to come into my heart, take control of my life, and make me the kind of person that You want me to be. Thank You for coming into my life as You promised. Amen."

Acknowledgments

This book has been a team effort before a word of it was ever written. It was written in my heart by all who have mentored me in life through taking time to lovingly teach me; even when I didn't recognize my own ignorance.

I thank and praise the Lord for all of the "Barnabas" encouragers whom He has brought into my life.

Thank You, Lord, for parents and grandparents who provided both Dave and me with foundational instruction in godly living when we were youngsters.

Thank You, Lord, for our own children whose lives continue to exhort me in pursuing godliness.

Thank You, Lord, for my husband Dave's enthusiastic support, insightful ideas, and selfless patience when I was "in the zone" while writing.

Thank You, Lord, for the staff at the Camarillo Evangelical Free Church who gave me the freedom and encouragement to write and teach this Bible study.

Thank You, Lord, for the hundreds of women whose lives have been transformed through walking the Ancient Paths. Their lives have urged me on, and they have lovingly helped me with their suggestions and passion for biblical accuracy. These women have helped to prepare this study for publication.

Thank You, Lord, for servants like Pat Papenhausen whose tireless efforts to edit this series have yielded much fruit. For Elaine Lucas and Linda Campbell, who have been true cheerleaders in initiating and facilitating the teaching of Ancient Paths for Modern Women. For Leigh Anne Tsuji's expertise and commitment to enhancing the fruitfulness of this ministry. For Laurie Donahue, whose vision and impetus is making these materials become widely available to women.

Thank You, Lord, for Your gifted servants, Dr. Howard Hendricks and Nancy Leigh DeMoss, who selflessly encouraged me more than they will ever know.

Lord, thank You. May these study materials help the women of our generation find "rest for their souls" as they return to the Ancient Paths. This study is from You ... use it for Your purposes and pleasure.

**"For from Him and through Him and to Him are all things.
To Him be the glory forever. Amen."
Romans 11:36.**

About the Author

 Judy Gerry met the Lord Jesus Christ as her Savior when she was a young child. During her college years at the University of California at Riverside, Judy received training through the ministry of Campus Crusade for Christ. She attended their Institute of Biblical Studies where she received in-depth Bible training from some of the nation's top seminary professors. Those classes piqued her hunger for the Word of God.

In 1969 she graduated and joined the staff of Campus Crusade for Christ. She married Dave Gerry in 1971. By 1979, their lives were bustling as the parents of five youngsters. Realizing that children are a blessing from God, Dave and Judy relished the opportunity to love and train their children. Judy's greatest desire has always been to please the Lord by being a godly wife and mother. Today, all of their grown children are believers, and Judy and Dave agree that, "I have no greater joy than this, to hear of my children walking in the truth" (III John 4).

Judy and Dave were active on the board of directors for Child Evangelism Fellowship in Denver, Colorado, in the 1980s, and they were enthusiastic AWANA directors for many years. Judy continues to be active in her local "Moms-in-Touch" prayer group and mentoring "Mothers of Preschoolers."

She has been teaching and writing Bible studies for over thirty years. Her great delight is seeing believers experience the blessings of intimacy with the Lord, and victory in their lives, as they obediently follow God's "ancient paths" (Jeremiah 6:16).

Judy and Dave are enjoying their empty-nest years in Camarillo, California, as they mentor young families in their church, teach Bible studies, speak at retreats, delight in their grandchildren, and daily anticipate the return of the Lord Jesus Christ.

Ancient Paths Ministries

Ancient Paths Ministries is committed to redirecting contemporary culture back to the timeless truths of God's Word.

With an emphasis on the practical application of Scripture to everyday living, Dave and Judy Gerry provide Bible studies and resources for spiritual growth and maturity. As authors, Bible teachers, and conference speakers, they exhort others to pursue Jesus Christ and to know Him. It is through nurturing that relationship that one will discover the foundation of all issues of life. In addition to speaking at men's and women's conferences, Dave and Judy also lead challenging weekend marriage retreats on, "How to Have an Intentional Marriage."

For more information contact:

Dave and Judy Gerry
P.O. Box 498
Somis, CA 93066
(805) 484-2808

E-mail: Judy@AncientPathsMinsitries.com
www.AncientPathsMinistries.com

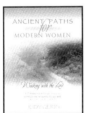
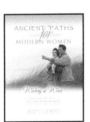
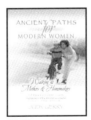